GOOD KING WENCESLAS
PRIMO

Arranged by
Marion Marwick and Maryanne Nagy

O COME ALL YE FAITHFUL

SECONDO

Arranged by
Marion Marwick and Maryanne Nagy

GOOD KING WENCESLAS

SECONDO

*Arranged by Marion Marwick and Maryanne Nagy

*For our students at Creative Keyboards

Duets for Chistmas

Arranged by Marion Marwick and Maryanne Nagy

Recital Series for Piano

*Good King Wencelas • O Come All Ye Faithful
Silent Night • The First Noel • Away in a Manger*

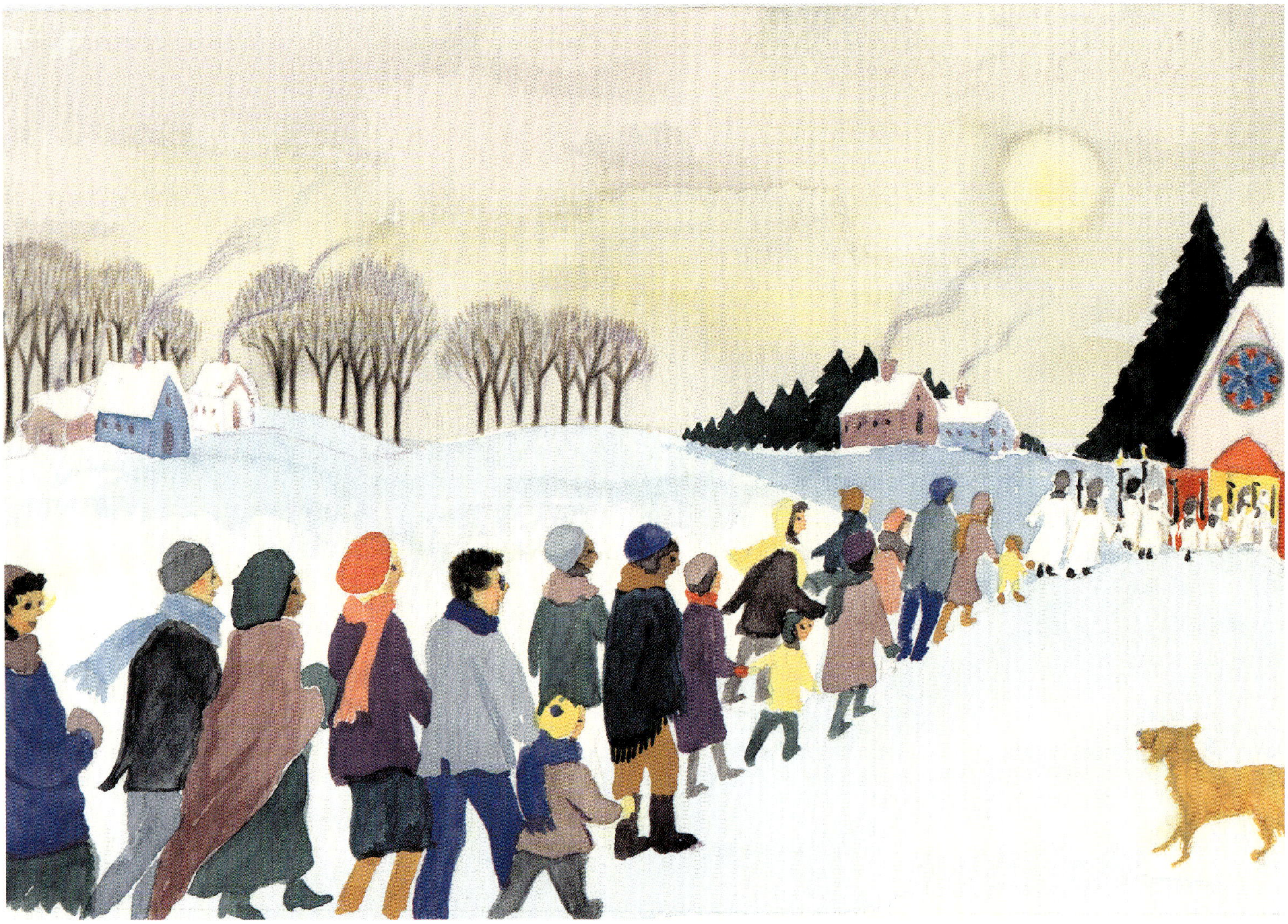

Edited by Robert Pace

Lee Roberts Music Publications Inc.
Chatham, New York

O COME ALL YE FAITHFUL

PRIMO

Arranged by
Marion Marwick and Maryanne Nagy

SILENT NIGHT
SECONDO

Arranged by
Marion Marwick and Maryanne Nagy

SILENT NIGHT

PRIMO

Arranged by
Marion Marwick and Maryanne Nagy

©Copyright 1972 by LEE ROBERTS MUSIC PUBLICATIONS, Inc.
International Copyright Secured   Made in U.S.A.   All Rights Reserved

THE FIRST NOEL
PRIMO

Arranged by
Marion Marwick and Maryanne Nagy

©Copyright 1972 by LEE ROBERTS MUSIC PUBLICATIONS, Inc.
International Copyright Secured   Made in U.S.A.   All Rights Reserved

AWAY IN A MANGER

SECONDO

Arranged by
Marion Marwick and Maryanne Nagy

AWAY IN A MANGER

PRIMO

Arranged by
Marion Marwick and Maryanne Nagy

©Copyright 1972 by LEE ROBERTS MUSIC PUBLICATIONS, Inc.
International Copyright Secured   Made in U.S.A.   All Rights Reserved

U.S. $3.95
ISBN 0-6340-3951-2

HL00372283